Barracudas

by Colleen Sexton

BELLWETHER MEDIA • MINNEAPOLIS, MN

E
597.7
SEX

Note to Librarians, Teachers, and Parents:

Blastoff! Readers are carefully developed by literacy experts and combine standards-based content with developmentally appropriate text.

Level 1 provides the most support through repetition of high-frequency words, light text, predictable sentence patterns, and strong visual support.

Level 2 offers early readers a bit more challenge through varied simple sentences, increased text load, and less repetition of high-frequency words.

Level 3 advances early-fluent readers toward fluency through increased text and concept load, less reliance on visuals, longer sentences, and more literary language.

Level 4 builds reading stamina by providing more text per page, increased use of punctuation, greater variation in sentence patterns, and increasingly challenging vocabulary.

Level 5 encourages children to move from "learning to read" to "reading to learn" by providing even more text, varied writing styles, and less familiar topics.

Whichever book is right for your reader, Blastoff! Readers are the perfect books to build confidence and encourage a love of reading that will last a lifetime!

This edition first published in 2010 by Bellwether Media, Inc.

No part of this publication may be reproduced in whole or in part without written permission of the publisher. For information regarding permission, write to Bellwether Media, Inc., Attention: Permissions Department, 5357 Penn Avenue South, Minneapolis, MN 55419.

Library of Congress Cataloging-in-Publication Data
Sexton, Colleen A., 1967-
  Barracudas / by Colleen Sexton.
     p. cm. – (Blastoff! readers. Oceans alive)
  Includes bibliographical references and index.
  Summary: "Simple text and full-color photographs introduce beginning readers to barracudas. Developed by literacy experts for students in kindergarten through third grade"–Provided by publisher.
  ISBN 978-1-60014-270-3 (hardcover : alk. paper)
  1. Barracudas–Juvenile literature. I. Title.

QL638.S77S49 2010
597.7–dc22   2009008184

Text copyright © 2010 by Bellwether Media, Inc. BLASTOFF! READERS and associated logos are trademarks and/or registered trademarks of Bellwether Media, Inc. SCHOLASTIC, CHILDREN'S PRESS, and associated logos are trademarks and/or registered trademarks of Scholastic Inc.

Printed in the United States of America, North Mankato, MN.   110110   1178

Contents

Barracudas are fish. They live in warm ocean waters around the world.

Some barracudas swim together in **schools**. Most barracudas swim alone.

There are more than 20 kinds of barracudas. The smallest are about 12 inches (31 centimeters) long.

Most barracudas are large.
The great barracuda can grow to
be 6 feet (2 meters) long.

A barracuda has a long, narrow body and a flat, pointed head.

8

The top of the body is a dark color. The sides and belly are light colors.

Some barracudas have dark spots, stripes, or other markings.

Barracudas have small **scales** all over their bodies.

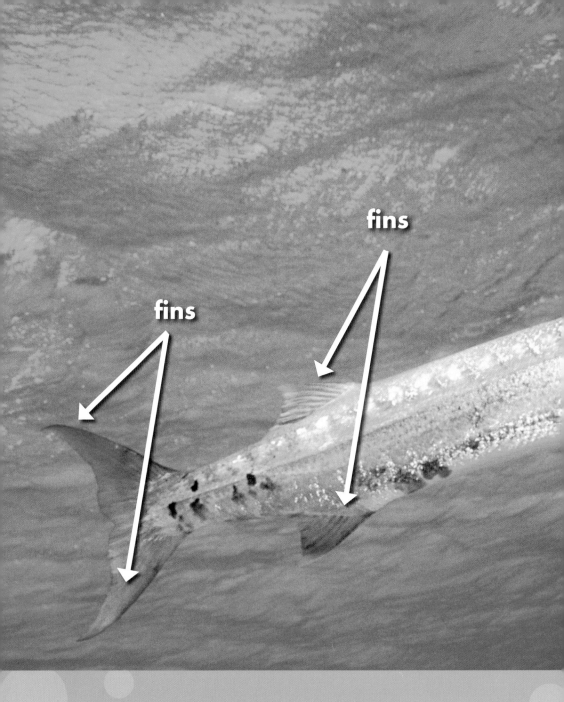

fins

fins

Barracudas have **fins**.
They move their fins back
and forth to swim and steer.

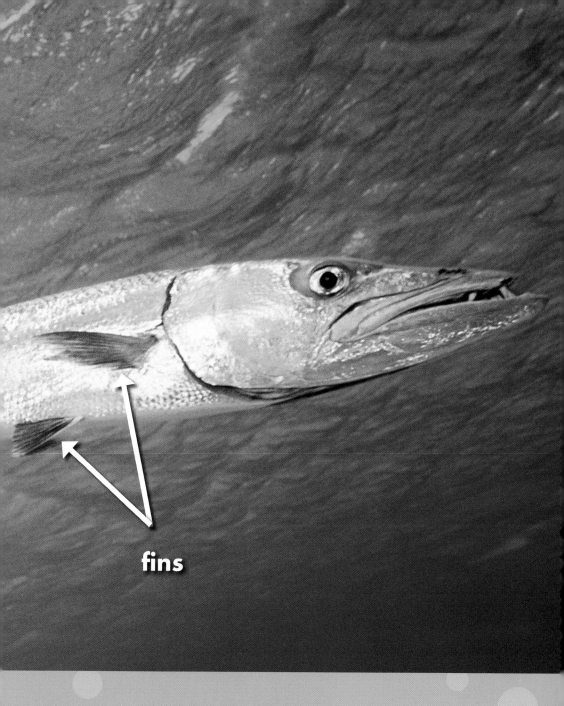

fins

Two large fins on a barracuda's tail help it speed through the water.

A barracuda's eyes are
near the top of its head.

gills

Barracudas breathe through **gills**.

Barracudas have wide mouths filled with long, sharp teeth. Their lower jaws stick out.

Barracudas sleep during the day and hunt at night.

Barracudas swim near the surface to look for herring, groupers, grunts, and other fish to eat.

18

They also hunt in **coral reefs**.

Barracudas move fast when they spot **prey**.

Chomp! A barracuda grabs a fish with its teeth. Then it begins to look for its next meal.

Glossary

coral reef—a structure in the ocean made of the skeletons of small, tube-shaped animals called corals

fins—the parts of a fish used to move, steer, and stop in the water

gills—organs on a fish's body that it uses to breathe; gills move oxygen from the water to the fish's blood.

prey—an animal that is hunted by another animal for food

scales—plate-like coverings on the bodies of many fish; barracudas have soft, round scales.

school—a large group of fish that swim and feed together

To Learn More

AT THE LIBRARY
Coldiron, Deborah. *Barracuda*. Edina, Minn.: ABDO, 2009.

Nuzzolo, Deborah. *Barracudas*. Mankato, Minn.: Capstone, 2009.

Sill, Cathryn. *About Fish: A Guide for Children*. Atlanta, Ga.: Peachtree, 2002.

ON THE WEB
Learning more about barracudas is as easy as 1, 2, 3.

1. Go to www.factsurfer.com.

2. Enter "barracudas" into the search box.

3. Click the "Surf" button and you will see a list of related Web sites.

With factsurfer.com, finding more information is just a click away.

Index

The images in this book are reproduced through the courtesy of: Richard Brooks, front cover, p. 20; Carlos Estape / imagequestmarine.com, pp. 4-5; Wolfgang Pölzer / Alamy, p. 6; Reinhard Dirscherl / age fotostock, pp. 7, 14-15; Ilya D. Gridnev, pp. 8-9; Sergey Popov V, pp. 10-11; David Nardini / Masterfile, pp. 12-13; imagebroker / Alamy, pp. 16-17; Stephen Frink / Getty Images, p. 18; Chris A Crumley / Alamy, p. 19; Mark Conlin / V&W / imagequestmarine.com, p. 21.